Does the Bible Predict the Future?

Ralph O. Muncaster

HARVEST HOUSE PUBLISHERS
Eugene, Oregon 97402

Cover by Terry Dugan Design, Minneapolis, Minnesota

By Ralph O. Muncaster

Can Archaeology Prove the New Testament?
Can We Know for Certain We Are Going To Heaven?
Can You Trust The Bible?
Creation vs. Evolution
Creation vs. Evolution *Video
Does Prayer Really Work?
Does the Bible Predict the Future?
How Do We Know Jesus Is God?
How is Jesus Different from Other Religious Leaders?
How to Talk About Jesus With the Skeptics in Your Life
Is The Bible Really A Message From God?
Science - Was the Bible Ahead of It's Time?
What is the Proof For the Resurrection?
What is the Trinity?
What Really Happened Christmas Morning?
What Really Happens When You Die?
Why Does God Allow Suffering?

DOES THE BIBLE PREDICT THE FUTURE?
Copyright © 2000 by Ralph O. Muncaster
Published by Harvest House Publishers
Eugene, Oregon 97402

Library of Congress Cataloging-in-Publication Data

Muncaster, Ralph O.
    Does the Bible predict the future? / Ralph O. Muncaster.
        p. cm. — (Examine the evidence series)
    ISBN 0-7369-0353-4
        1. Bible—Prophecies. I. Title.

BS647.2 .M86 2000
220.1'5—dc21   00-024157

Printed in the United States of America.

02 03 04 05 06 07 08 09 / BP / 10 9 8 7 6 5 4 3 2

Contents

Why Is Prophecy Important? 4

The Key Issues 6

Prophecy "Proof" of God 8

The Importance of Perfect Prophecy 10

How the Bible Fits with History 12

Prophecy Overview—The Books of Moses 14

Prophecy Overview—The Books of History and Literature 16

Prophecy Overview—The Books of the Prophets 18

Prophecy Overview—The Books of the New Testament 20

The Life of Jesus: Foretold by Prophecy 22

1500 Years of Prophecies of Christ 24

Prophecies of Jesus' Final Week 26

Jesus' Own Prophecies 28

Prophecy Models of Jesus 30

Proof: Prophecies About Christ Were Not Contrived 32

Prophecies of Israel and the Jews 34

Israel and the Jews—Prophecies of Exile 36

Prophecy Examples—People 38

Prophecy Examples—Places 40

Prophecy Examples—Events 42

Common Questions 44

Notes 48

Bibliography 48

Why Is Prophecy Important?

Mankind is obsessed with the future.

Relationships . . . career . . . health . . . fortune . . . death . . . questions about the future dominate people's thinking. The three basic forms of predicting the future (other than guessing) are:

> *Forecasting* (by experts)—Predictions of effects from causes—based on experience and understanding (encouraged by the Bible).

> *Divination* (by psychics and others)—Predictions based on supernatural information not from God (forbidden by the Bible).

> *Prophecy* (by prophets)—Predictions based on information received from God (recommended by and contained within the Bible).

Experts can be wrong. Psychics are frequently wrong. Prophets are never, *never* wrong. So seriously was the role of biblical prophets taken that they were put to death upon making a single error in a prophecy.

The importance of prophecy is stressed in the Bible with commands to:

1. *Test everything* . . . including holy books and people (see pages 10,11).

2. *Use prophecy* . . . to determine if something is from God (see pages 8–11).

The Bible is both open to and available for the testing of prophecy. More than 1000 prophecies fill the Bible. These prophecies are about people, places, and events—precise prophecies made centuries in advance of their fulfillment.

We can choose to accept or reject the message of the Bible. Doctors tell us how to extend our lives, and engineers tell us how to build bridges. We commonly accept advice from such experts. Yet engineers and doctors are sometimes wrong. The Bible tells us how to achieve a full life on earth and for eternity. Prophecy helps verify that the Bible is *never* wrong. We would be foolish to reject it.

Human Standards of Success

- Have a 40-percent hitting average in professional baseball.

- Successfully predict winners of football games 75 percent of the time over one season.

- Flip a coin 100 times and correctly predict heads or tails 60 percent of the time.

- Predict correctly the winning candidate in three of the next four U.S. presidential elections.

- In 100 different comparisons of two very similar stocks, correctly select the best-performing one over a 12-month period 70 percent of the time.

God's Standard of Success

- 100 percent—absolutely no errors in any prophecy, no matter how miraculous or incredible it might seem.

- One mistake by a prophet was to be punished by death.

The Key Issues

Have you ever "known" an answer you shouldn't have known? Or had an experience you feel "certain" occurred before (déjà vu)? Most people claim to have had such experiences. The entire process of thought raises many questions. Where do thoughts come from? Are they all "self-generated"? Or can thoughts come from sources outside the domain of time and space?

Prophecy deals with foretelling future events. Yet biblical prophets had a far greater role. They were also interpreters of divine messages that were used to guide and direct the leaders of Israel. In order to separate such divine inspiration from other "supernatural" messages, God instructed the Jews to *execute* anyone who gave false prophecy (Deuteronomy 18:20-22).

Understanding prophecy involves the following key issues:

1. Is Supernatural Communication Real?

People have been known to provide information that seems to defy the odds. It may indicate supernatural origin. Universities studying ESP have sometimes found evidence that seems to suggest supernatural sources, though these sources always also give many wrong answers.[3] Prophecy in the Bible is *unique in its total accuracy*. Such accuracy is a statistical impossibility without God (see pages 8–21).

2. How Do We Know Messages Are from God?

Recognizing the existence of false prophets and other potential supernatural sources of information, God provided specific instructions to "test everything" (1 Thessalonians 5:20,21). In the realm of prophecy, anything not 100-percent accurate is not from God (Deuteronomy 18:22; Isaiah 41:22,23—see pages 8–11,44,45 in this book).

3. What Do We Do As a Result?

Analysis will reveal that the Bible is the only reliable source of prophecy from God. And God commanded against other attempts of divination (Deuteronomy 18:10-13). The correct action is to follow the biblical guidelines (see pages 22–31, 44–47).

The "Prophecy Source" Test

	YES	NO
1. Does the source contain any prophecies at all?	☐	☐
2. If so, can the prophecies be verified by actual events, or are they just "hopes" or "wishes" about the future?	☐	☐
3. Are the source's prophecies 100-percent accurate?	☐	☐
4. Are the source's prophecies specific and detailed?	☐	☐
5. Are the source's prophecies meaningful?	☐	☐

Supernatural Communication— Which of These Are from God?

Astrology?
Psychics?
Numerology?
Ouija board?
Tarot cards?
Vinaya Pitaka?
Abidhamma Pitaka?
Sutta Pitaka?
The Vedas?
The Upanishads?
Ramayana?
Mahabharata?
Bhagavad Gita?
The Puranas?
The Five Classics?
The Tao Te King?
Ko-ji-ki?
Nihongi?
Avesta?
Qur'an?
Granth Sahib?
Humanist Manifesto?
The Book of Mormon?
Doctrine and Covenants?
Pearl of Great Price?
The Divine Principle?
Science and Health?
The Watchtower?

The Bible?

Prophecy "Proof" of God

Can we ever "prove" anything? Apart from mathematical proofs, many critics would say no, especially regarding history or even regarding the world around us.

However, statisticians and most other scientists agree there is a point when the probability of something happening is so remote that it becomes absurd or essentially impossible. As a guideline, scientists accept that anything with a probability of less than one chance in 10^{50} (1 followed by 50 zeros) is "impossible." If such an "impossible" event happens to occur, it may be concluded that it required God's action or some other supernatural action outside of the dimensions of time and space.

For example, suppose a friend correctly foretold the winning number in a state lottery with one single prediction (like buying *one* ticket). The odds of that are about one in 10,000,000 (or 1 in 10^7). You might be extremely impressed, but you probably wouldn't claim he had "divine insight." Now suppose he did it a second consecutive time—again with one single prediction. The odds immediately jump to one in 100,000,000,000,000 (1 in 10^{14}). Suddenly it would seem impossible without some trick or supernatural information. Imagine someone successfully picking three consecutive lotteries (one chance in 10^{21}). Such an "impossible" feat would likely end lotteries forever—because the odds of such a chance occurrence are nil.

The miraculous insights in the Bible occurring by chance has a probability far more remote than that of winning *dozens* of lotteries in the manner described above. Only supernatural inspiration can account for it. "Statistical proof" of God's inspiration comes in at least three ways:

Scientific insights—Scientific information in the Bible that was written hundreds, even thousands of years before modern science had the knowledge to recognize the Bible was correct. These insights are in the areas of physics, biology, engineering, and medicine, among others (see *Science—Was the Bible Ahead of Its Time?* in the *Examine the Evidence* series).

Concealed evidence—Cross-referenced information contained in books of the Bible that were written hundreds of years apart by very different authors in different situations in different parts of the world.

Prophecy miracles—The future foretold with precision and total accuracy. Over 1000 specific prophecies are recorded in the Bible, of which 668 are historical.[14] None have errors. All types of prophecies are included—about people, places, and events. Irrefutable evidence exists that these prophecies could *not* have been contrived (see pages 32,33).

Probability Comparison

1 in 10^7 .... Correct Prediction of 1 Lottery

1 in 10^7 .... **Prophecies of Tyre** (see page 40)

1 in 10^{14} .... Correct Prediction of 2 Consecutive Lotteries

1 in 10^{14} .... **Prophecy of Cyrus** (see page 38)

1 in 10^{154} .... Correct Prediction of 22 Consecutive Lotteries

1 in 10^{157} ..... **Just 48 of the prophecies8 of Christ** (see pages 13–18)

1 in 10^{999} **+** .... Correct Prediction of More Than 100 Consecutive Lotteries

1 in 10^{999} + ... **All Biblical Prophecies***

*Note: Beyond all reason without God's involvement

The Importance of Perfect Prophecy

How important is prophecy? Some people might believe that prophecy is interesting, but is not especially important. Nothing could be further from the truth.

> *Prophecy is a key standard the Bible tells us to use to "test" whether something is truly from God (Deuteronomy 18:19-22).*

This standard is obviously critical. It means that words spoken, writings, and information of all types that are claimed to be from God should be judged based on any prophecies made. If a holy book is supposed to be inspired by God, it must be 100-percent accurate regarding all prophecies. This is a big problem for the holy books of some religions (see page 44,45).

> *Only the Bible commands its readers to "test everything" (1 Thessalonians 5:21).*
>
> *Only the Bible is 100-percent accurate in hundreds of specific prophecies.*

How accurate is biblical prophecy? As indicated below, hundreds of specific *historical* prophecies have already been verified exactly as predicted in the Bible. Many were fulfilled in the lifetimes of the prophets. Others were fulfilled centuries later. Of the Bible's historical prophecies, all but three have been verified as being fulfilled. (This does not mean these three were not fulfilled—just that we have no confirmation of their fulfillment.)

The choice of prophecy by God to verify His involvement in history is significant. Many people seem to think miracles are the strongest evidence of God. Yet the Bible tells us that Satan "masquerades as an angel of light" (2 Corinthians 11:14). The

The Bible's Prophecies[14]

SUMMARY	OLD TESTAMENT	NEW TESTAMENT	TOTAL	
Historically fulfilled	467	201	668	68%
Fulfillment not confirmed	2*	1*	3*	<1%
Heaven or second coming (to be fulfilled)	105	237	342	32%
Total	574	439	1013	

Note: Count of prophecies is limited to distinct references.[2,14] Breaking prophecies into parts or adding model-type prophecies would increase the number considerably.

* Unknown fulfillment: Jeremiah 35:1-19; 49:1-6; John 1:40-51

Bible also describes many counterfeit miracles *not* performed by God that were used to deceive people (for example, Exodus 7:11,12; 2 Thessalonians 2:9). Hence, even "good" miracles—including healing and other helpful occurrences—are not necessarily from God.

Types of Prophecy

Confusion can exist due to the nature of various prophecies. Some are quite specific and to the point (for example, "Cyrus" on page 38). Others are "veiled," requiring insight and understanding provided by the Holy Spirit (for example, Genesis 3:15—see pages 14,15). And some prophecies have dual meanings (often a short-term and a later meaning). Biblical prophecy as a whole is unmistakable evidence of God's influence. Detailed study can reveal even more insights.

How the Bible Fits with History

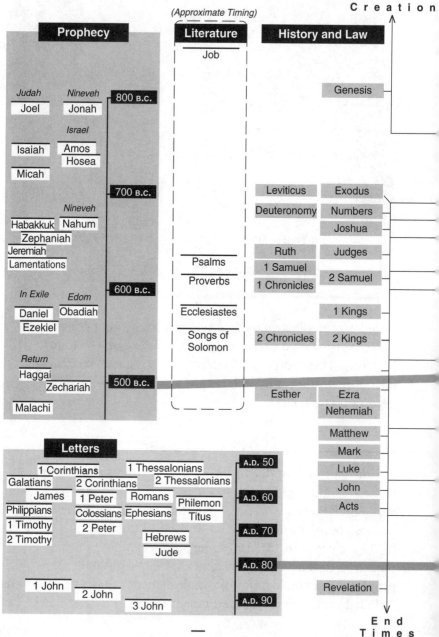

(Approximate Timing)

Creation

Prophecy	Literature	History and Law

Job

Genesis

| *Judah* | *Nineveh* | 800 B.C. |
| Joel | Jonah | |

Israel

Isaiah	Amos
	Hosea
Micah	

700 B.C.

Leviticus — Exodus
Deuteronomy — Numbers
Joshua

Nineveh
Habakkuk — Nahum
Zephaniah
Jeremiah
Lamentations

Ruth — Judges
Psalms
1 Samuel
Proverbs — 2 Samuel
1 Chronicles

600 B.C.

In Exile   *Edom*
Daniel — Obadiah
Ezekiel

Ecclesiastes — 1 Kings

Songs of Solomon — 2 Chronicles — 2 Kings

Return
Haggai
Zechariah

500 B.C.

Esther — Ezra
Nehemiah

Malachi

Matthew

Letters

Mark

1 Corinthians   1 Thessalonians — A.D. 50
Galatians   2 Corinthians   2 Thessalonians

Luke

James   Romans   John
1 Peter   Philemon   A.D. 60
Philippians   Colossians Ephesians   Titus   Acts
1 Timothy   2 Peter
2 Timothy   A.D. 70

Hebrews
Jude

A.D. 80

1 John   Revelation
2 John
3 John   A.D. 90

End Times

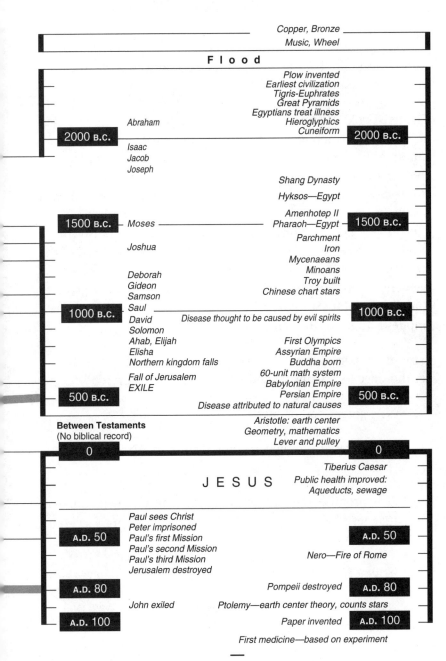

Copper, Bronze
Music, Wheel

F l o o d

Plow invented
Earliest civilization
Tigris-Euphrates
Great Pyramids
Egyptians treat illness
Abraham
Hieroglyphics
Cuneiform

2000 B.C. — 2000 B.C.

Isaac
Jacob
Joseph

Shang Dynasty

Hyksos—Egypt

Amenhotep II
1500 B.C. — Moses — Pharaoh—Egypt — 1500 B.C.

Parchment
Joshua
Iron
Mycenaeans
Deborah
Minoans
Gideon
Troy built
Samson
Chinese chart stars
Saul
1000 B.C. — 1000 B.C.
David — Disease thought to be caused by evil spirits
Solomon
Ahab, Elijah
First Olympics
Elisha
Assyrian Empire
Northern kingdom falls
Buddha born
60-unit math system
Fall of Jerusalem
Babylonian Empire
EXILE
Persian Empire
500 B.C. — 500 B.C.
Disease attributed to natural causes

Between Testaments
Aristotle: earth center
(No biblical record)
Geometry, mathematics
Lever and pulley
0 — 0

Tiberius Caesar
J E S U S — Public health improved:
Aqueducts, sewage

Paul sees Christ
Peter imprisoned
A.D. 50 — Paul's first Mission — A.D. 50
Paul's second Mission
Paul's third Mission — Nero—Fire of Rome
Jerusalem destroyed

A.D. 80 — A.D. 80
Pompeii destroyed
John exiled
Ptolemy—earth center theory, counts stars
A.D. 100 — Paper invented — A.D. 100

First medicine—based on experiment

Prophecy Overview
The Books of Moses

Almost every book of the Bible contains prophecy. Sixteen Old Testament books have specific prophecy about Christ.

The five books of Moses (the Torah) contain about 60 prophecies, at least 15 of which refer to a coming Messiah. The very first prophecy in Genesis warns of God's judgment: that eating from the tree of the knowledge of good and evil will cause death (Genesis 2:16,17). The second prophecy responds to the first with a veiled reference to God's plan of redemption (Genesis 3:15). The offspring of the woman (Christ) will ultimately "crush the head" of the serpent (Satan). Even the biblical phrase "seed of the woman" refers to divine conception. "Seed" refers to the male element of reproduction, which in the case of Christ was given to Mary by the Holy Spirit, not by a man. "Seed of the woman" implies a virgin birth (Matthew 1:18; Luke 1:34,35).

Genesis contains a number of other important prophecies that set the stage for the most significant events in history:

- The great flood (Genesis 6:7)

- The covenant to bless the world through Abraham (Genesis 12:3)

- The promise of Palestine to Abraham and his descendants (Genesis 12:7)

- Isaac's "sacrifice"—a prophecy of the resurrection (see page 31; Genesis 22)

- The identification of Christ's ancestors (Genesis 22:18; 49:10-12)

Probability Comparison—
The Bible's Prophecies vs. Predicting Coin Flips

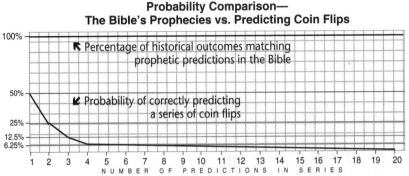

The probability of correctly predicting the outcome of a series of ten coin flips is .1 percent, or one chance in approximately 1000. The probability of correctly predicting a series of 20 coin flips is .0001 percent, or one chance in approximately *10 trillion.*

The Bible's accuracy is *perfect* over a series of *hundreds* of historically verifiable prophecies—and most of these prophecies have an outcome *far more* complex than the simple one-out-of-two outcome of a coin flip.

Other prophecies in the Torah contain a great deal of specific information that has subsequently shaped our world. Such things as the age-old conflict in the Middle East can be traced to prophecies about each of Abraham's sons. Ishmael was a son of Abraham through his maidservant, Hagar (an Egyptian). Although Ishmael's birth was not ordained by God, God promised that he would become a great nation (Genesis 21:13,18). The Arab nations are the result. Isaac, the child promised by God, was also prophesied to become a great nation (Israel). Not surprisingly, the conflict began in Abraham's time. Discord between Abraham's wife Sarah and Hagar forced Hagar and Ishmael to move away (Genesis 21:8-21).

It is significant that the many prophecies about the promise of the land of Canaan to Abraham were written by Moses in the desert *before* entering the "promised land." Moses died before the Jews entered Canaan. Ironically, the reason the Jews were forced to spend 40 years in the desert in the first place was because they questioned the original prophecy of God which promised them the land. Of the original Jews of the Exodus from Egypt, only Caleb and Joshua, who fully accepted earlier prophecy, entered Canaan (Numbers 14:20-35).

Prophecy Overview
The Books of History and Literature

The other *historical* books of the Old Testament contain nearly 100 prophecies, mostly regarding impending events contemporary to the recording of the prophecies.

Prophecy in the Promised Land

Joshua became the leader of the Israelites as they entered the promised land. It's not surprising that Joshua prayed for guidance from God and believed God's prophecies, since he was one of the two people who believed God's earlier promise of the land to Abraham. Prophecies in the Book of Joshua include reiteration of the promise of the land (Joshua 1:1-9), and victories over Jericho (Joshua 6:1-50), Ai (Joshua 8:1), the Amorites (Joshua 10:7,8), and the northern kings (Joshua 11:6).

The books of Judges, Samuel (two books), Kings (two books) and Chronicles (two books) contain prophecies of military victories of kings (Saul, David, and Solomon) and of many miscellaneous details (for example, prediction of specific births, deaths, and events). Two of Israel's greatest prophets, Elijah and Elisha, neither of whom has a specific book of prophecy, were active during this period. Prophecies in the historical books are extremely specific. Examples include:

- The sons of Eli were to die on the same day (1 Samuel 2:34)

- Saul was to be chosen as king (1 Samuel 9:15,16)

- David was to kill Goliath (1 Samuel 17:45-47)

- Bathsheba's child was to die (2 Samuel 12:14)

- Three days of plagues for Israel (2 Samuel 24:12-14;
  1 Chronicles 21:1-13)

- A drought was to occur (1 Kings 17:1)

- The drought was to end with rain promised at Elijah's request (1 Kings 18:41)

- Jezebel was to be eaten by dogs (1 Kings 21:23)

- Gehazi was to be afflicted with leprosy (2 Kings 5:27)

- A seven-year famine was to come to Israel (2 Kings 8:1)

The Psalms and Books of Literature

One might expect the Psalms to contain many prophecies since they were usually composed in times of great emotion and spiritual awareness. And in fact, the Psalms contain nearly 100 prophecies, mostly written by David about 1000 B.C. Many of the prophecies actually include several elements (for example, Psalm 22 contains over a dozen prophetic references to Christ's crucifixion). Prophecies in the Psalms sometimes have dual meanings or purposes—perhaps relating both to a situation David is facing and also making a veiled reference to an important future event. About one-third of the prophecies in the Psalms refer to the coming Messiah.

Proverbs and Ecclesiastes contain little prophecy other than indirect references. The book of Job may be the oldest book in the Bible, and it contains interesting prophetic insight.

The Book of Job

The book of Job contains some amazing insights, especially considering that it was written some 2000 years before Christ. It prophesies the coming of Christ, the resurrection of the body, and eternal life with God (Job 19:25-27).

Prophecy Overview
The Books of the Prophets

About one-third of the prophecies contained in the Bible are in the books of the prophets, wich were written from about 800 B.C. to about 400 B.C. Even the arrival of the prophets was prophesied by Moses (Deuteronomy 18:15). The role of prophets was not simply to foretell the future, but also to provide instruction to other people from God. If a prophet made a single error, he was immediately executed. Holy Scripture came only from the words of a prophet who was shown *never* to be incorrect. Ironically, some prophets were executed despite their accuracy since God's messages were often unpopular and frequently caused violent reactions (for example, 2 Chronicles 24:20-22).

The Books of Prophecy

The earliest books of prophecy are Joel, written in Judah about 800 B.C.; and Jonah, written in Nineveh about 770 B.C. Plagues were prophesied (and occurred) in Joel's lifetime; he also made prophecies about the end of time. Jonah prophesied about the destruction of Nineveh (which occurred in 612 B.C.)

Isaiah is considered one of the greatest prophets. The Book of Isaiah, written in Judah in about 700 B.C., is one of the Bible's most important books of prophecy. Isaiah contains more prophecies than any writing of the period except Jeremiah. It also contains 1) the *most prophecies about Christ* and 2) the *most detailed prophecy of Christ* (in chapter 53). Some of the prophecies in Isaiah include:

- The prophecy of John the Baptist (40:1-5)

- The birth of Christ and His impact (9:1-7)

- A virgin birth, in anticipation of Christ's virgin birth (7:14-16)

- Prophecies about many cities and regions

- The prophecy that Cyrus would rebuild Jerusalem and the temple (44:28—see page 38).

About the time that Isaiah was prophesying in the southern kingdom of Judah, Amos and Hosea were active in the northern kingdom of Israel. Prophecies of Amos contain harsh messages of judgment. Hosea's prophecies focus more on restoration and God's love to people, even sinful people. Following Hosea was Micah, who wrote to both kingdoms. In addition to prophecy of the exile and return, Micah prophesied the city of Bethlehem as the birthplace of the Messiah (Micah 5:1-4).

The lesser-known prophets Nahum (who prophesied about Nineveh), Obadiah (who prophesied about Edom), and Habakkuk and Zephaniah (who prophesied about Judah) gave prophecies of judgment during the middle to early 600s B.C. Also during the preexile period, Jeremiah spoke forth over 80 prophecies, providing a number of details of the judgment awaiting Judah. History later confirmed all of this—even to the smallest detail, including the duration of the exile (Jeremiah 25:9-11; 29:10-14).

During the exile (587 B.C.–517 B.C.) Ezekiel and Daniel were active in Babylon. In addition to many exile prophecies, Ezekiel predicted the return from a *second* major exile—which occurred in 1948 with the formation of Israel (Ezekiel 37:21). Daniel provided one of the most important prophecies in the Bible by predicting the day that the Messiah would enter Jerusalem as a king (Daniel 9:20-27—see page 26).

The last prophets of the Old Testament, Haggai, Zechariah, and Malachi, all prophesied after the return from exile in Babylon. Much of the prophecy of these later prophets concerned the *second* coming of Jesus Christ, the establishment of a future kingdom, and the end of the world.

Prophecy Overview
The Books of the New Testament

Not surprisingly, Jesus Christ provided a majority of the prophecy in the New Testament. This is extremely significant when combined with the mandate by Jewish law for perfect accuracy regarding prophecy (see pages 28,29).

Because of the 100-percent accuracy of the historical prophecies made by Jesus, we would be well-advised to take all other prophecies (including those about heaven and hell) of Jesus very seriously.

Prophecies in the Gospels cover a broad range of topics. The miraculous births of John the Baptist (Luke 1:13) and Jesus (Luke 1:31) were both foretold. Zechariah, a priest and the father of John the Baptist, who prophesied his son's birth, would have faced execution if his prophecy of a son were not accurate. And, of course, there was no ultrasound to determine gender and no incentive for Zechariah to falsify prophecy (not to mention no incentive for months of "pretending" to be mute—as happened to Zechariah). Mary and Joseph also faced shame and possible death if the prophecy given to them was not accurate.

The prophecies of Jesus included many predictions concerning His death and resurrection (see pages 28,29), along with prophecies of contemporary events and also of the end of the world. Examples of other prophecies of Jesus include:

- Jesus' words would never pass away (Matthew 24:35; Luke 21:33)

- Lazarus' illness would glorify God (John 11:4)

- Lazarus would rise again (John 11:23)

- The temple would be destroyed—not one stone would be left on another (Matthew 24:2; Luke 21:6)

- That people would accept other false "christs" (John 5:43)

The Book of Acts and the 21 Epistles altogether contain about 120 prophecies, mostly about future events such as the second coming of Christ.

Revelation *alone* contains over 130 prophecies, mostly about a second coming of Christ and the end of the world. Understanding Revelation requires in-depth analysis.

Was Jesus Just a "Great Prophet"?

Some nonbelieving Jews and other people say that Jesus was a "great prophet," but that He was not the Messiah and not the Son of God.

Such a statement is self-contradictory. A prophet by definition had to be 100-percent accurate. Jesus gave prophecy indicating that He was both the Messiah and the Son of God. So if Jesus was a great prophet, He also had to be the Messiah and the Son of God. Otherwise, He was not a prophet.

Considering Jesus' track record on other easily verified prophecies, we would be wise to also believe His more significant claims (see pages 44–47).

The Life of Jesus: Foretold by Prophecy

The following describes the Messiah
only from Old Testament prophecy
(the numbers refer to the Scriptures in the box
on the opposite page)

The Messiah will descend from Shem,[1] Abraham,[2] Isaac,[3] Jacob,[4] Judah,[5] Jesse,[6] and King David.[7] He will be born in the city of Bethlehem in the county of Ephrathah[8] when a bright star appears.[9] It will be a miraculous, virgin birth.[10]

The Messiah will be unique, having preexisted His birth.[8] He will perform many miracles: calming the sea,[11] causing the blind to see, the deaf to hear, the lame to walk, and the mute to talk.[12] He will be referred to in many ways, including: God with us,[10] wonderful counselor, mighty God, everlasting Father, and prince of peace.[13] He will be a great teacher and will use parables.[14] One day He will rule over everything—all nations will bow down to Him.[15,22]

But the Messiah will come to save mankind.[16] He will become man's sin offering[16] and present Himself to Jerusalem as both the anointed King[18] and the Passover Lamb.[16] This will occur exactly 173,880* days after the decree by Artaxerxes to rebuild both Jerusalem and the temple.[17] So, on April 6, A.D. 32 the Messiah will present Himself to a rejoicing Jerusalem riding on a donkey.[18] But then He will suffer greatly.[16] He will be rejected by many, including His friends.[16] He

*An Incredible Prophecy!

Daniel 9:20-27 predicts *to the day* Jesus' entry into Jerusalem as king on a donkey. Appreciating this requires knowledge and understanding.[1,2,9,11,12]

will be betrayed by a friend[25] for 30 pieces of silver.[19] Later that money will be thrown on the floor of the temple[19] and will eventually go to a potter.[19] At His trial He will not defend Himself. He will say nothing[16] except as required by law. Israel will reject Him.[20]

The Messiah will be taken to a mountaintop identified by Abraham as "the Lord will provide."[21] There He will be crucified with His hands and feet pierced.[22] His enemies will encircle Him,[22] mocking Him, and will cast lots for His clothing.[22] He will call to God, asking why He was "forsaken."[22] He will be given gall and wine.[23] He will die with thieves.[16] But, unlike the thieves, none of His bones will be broken.[22] His heart will fail,[22] as indicated by blood and water spilling out[22] when He is pierced with a spear.[24] He will be buried in a rich man's grave.[16] In three days He will rise from the dead.[22]

Location of Prophecy

[1] Genesis 9–10
[2] Genesis 22:18
[3] Genesis 26:4
[4] Genesis 28:14
[5] Genesis 49:10
[6] Isaiah 11:1-5
[7] 2 Samuel 7:11-16
[8] Micah 5:2
[9] Numbers 24:17
[10] Isaiah 7:14
[11] Psalm 107:29
[12] Isaiah 35:4-6
[13] Isaiah 9:6
[14] Psalm 78:2
[15] Isaiah 45:23
[16] Isaiah 53:3-9
[17] Daniel 9:20-27
[18] Zechariah 9:9
[19] Zechariah 11:12,13
[20] Isaiah 8:14
[21] Genesis 22
[22] Psalm 22
[23] Psalm 69:20-22
[24] Zechariah 12:10
[25] Psalm 41:9

(partial listing)

23

1500 Years of Prophecies of Christ

Prophecy

✝ The eternal Christ (redeemer) lives, will come to earth, and will be victorious in the end

✝ Metaphorical prediction of Satan's attack on Christ ("striking heel") and Christ's ultimate victory

✝ Messiah to be descendant of Abraham

✝ Messiah to be descendant of Isaac

✝ Messiah to be descendant of Jacob

✝ Messiah to be from tribe of Judah

✝ No bones of Messiah to be broken

✝ Snake lifted in desert is a model (type) of Christ

✝ Prediction of Israel's greatness, the Messiah, and a "star" from the line of Jacob

✝ Christ to be "raised up" as a great prophet. Moses identified as a model (type)

✝ Christ to be hung on a tree becoming curse for us, redeeming us from original curse

✝ The body of Christ will not see decay

✝ Many details of suffering on cross. Crucifixion, mocking, casting lots for clothing

✝ False witnesses will accuse Christ

✝ Prediction that Christ will say "into your hands, I commit my spirit"

✝ No bones of Christ to be broken

✝ Christ to be hated without cause

✝ Friends will stay far away

✝ Christ will be betrayed by a friend

This is a partial list of the hundreds of prophetic references to the Messiah. It includes only selected historical prophecies (prophecies of Jesus' second coming are not included).

✝ Christ to be scorned by His enemies

✝ Christ to be given gall and vinegar

✝ Christ to be descendant of Solomon and rule forever

✝ Christ to speak in parables

✝ Some Jews ("the builders") will reject Christ—the "capstone"

✝ Christ to come from the line of David and rule forever

✝ The virgin birth of Christ anticipated

✝ Christ to perform miracles: make the blind see, the deaf hear, and the lame walk

✝ John the Baptist will be the forerunner of Christ

✝ Description of the coming Messiah

✝ Christ to be a light for the Gentiles and to bring salvation to the earth

✝ Christ will be obedient in His time of humiliation

✝ Many details foretold (for example, suffering servant; to be silent, crucified with evil, buried with rich)

✝ Christ to be called out of Egypt

✝ Christ will come from Bethlehem

✝ Christ will enter Jerusalem 173,880 days from the decree to rebuild the temple. He will then be crucifie and later Jerusalem will be destroyed

✝ Israel will welcome Christ, the Savior and king—who enters Jerusalem riding on a donkey

✝ Christ will be betrayed for 30 pieces of silver

✝ Christ to be pierced

Approximate Reference	Prophecy Timing	Given by	Place of Prophecy	Fulfillment
Job 19:25-27	2000 B.C.	Job	Mesopotamia	historical arrival of Christ
Genesis 3:15	1450 B.C.	Moses	Desert	Romans 16:20
Genesis 12:3	1450 B.C.	Moses	Desert	Matthew 1; Luke 3:23-37
Genesis 22:18; 26:4	1450 B.C.	Moses	Desert	Matthew 1; Luke 3:23-37
Genesis 28:14	1450 B.C.	Moses	Desert	Matthew 1; Luke 3:23-37
Genesis 49:10-12	1450 B.C.	Moses	Desert	Matthew 1; Luke 3:23-37
Exodus 12:46	1450 B.C.	Moses	Desert	John 19:31-36
Numbers 21:8,9	1450 B.C.	Moses	Desert	John 3:14,15
Numbers 24:17	1450 B.C.	Balaam	Desert	Matthew 2:2; Luke 1:33; Revelation 22:16
Deuteronomy 18:15-19	1450 B.C.	Moses	Desert	John 6:14; 7:40; Acts 3:22; 7:37
Deuteronomy 21:23	1450 B.C.	Moses	Desert	Galatians 3:13
Psalm 16:1-10	1000 B.C.	David	Palestine	Matthew 28; Acts 2:25-28; 13:35-37
Psalm 22	1000 B.C.	David	Palestine	Matthew 27; Mark 15; Luke 23; John 19
Psalm 27:12	1000 B.C.	David	Palestine	Matthew 26:59-61; Mark 14:57-59
Psalm 31:3-5	1000 B.C.	David	Palestine	Luke 23:46
Psalm 34:20	1000 B.C.	David	Palestine	John 19:36
Psalm 35:19	1000 B.C.	David	Palestine	John 15:24,25
Psalm 38:11	1000 B.C.	David	Palestine	Matthew 27:55; Mark 15:40; Luke 23:49
Psalm 41:9	1000 B.C.	David	Palestine	Matthew 26:14-16,47-50; Mark 14:17-21, Luke 22:21-23; John 13:18,19
Psalm 69:9,19	1000 B.C.	David	Palestine	Romans 15:3
Psalm 69:21	1000 B.C.	David	Palestine	Matthew 27:48; Mark 15:36; Luke 23:36
2 Samuel 7:13	930 B.C.	Samuel	Palestine	Matthew 1
Psalm 78:2	900 B.C.	Asaph	Palestine	Matthew 13:34,35
Psalm 118:22	Unknown	Unknown	Palestine	Matthew 21:42; Mark 12:10; Luke 20:17; Acts 4:11; 1 Peter 2:7
Psalm 132:11,12	Unknown	Unknown	Palestine	Matthew 1; Luke 3:23-37
Isaiah 7:14-16	700 B.C.	Isaiah	Judah	Matthew 1:20-23; Luke 1:34,35
Isaiah 35:4-6	700 B.C.	Isaiah	Judah	Matthew 15:30
Isaiah 40:1-5	681 B.C.	Isaiah	Judah	Matthew 3:1-3; Mark 1:2-4; Luke 1:76-79; John 1:23
Isaiah 42:1-13	681 B.C.	Isaiah	Judah	History
Isaiah 49:6	681 B.C.	Isaiah	Judah	Luke 2:32; Acts 13:47
Isaiah 50	681 B.C.	Isaiah	Judah	Matthew 27:30; Mark 14:65; 15:19,20; Luke 22:63-65
Isaiah 52:13-53	681 B.C.	Isaiah	Judah	Mark 15:3,4,27-32; Luke 23:1-25; John 1:29; 11:49-52; Acts 8:28-35; 10:43; 13:38,39; 1 Corinthians 15:3; Ephesians 1:7; 1 Peter 2:21-25; 1 John 1:7-9
Hosea 11:1	750 B.C.	Hosea	Israel	Matthew 2:14,15
Micah 5:1-4	700 B.C.	Micah	Judah	Matthew 2:1-6
Daniel 9:24-27	535 B.C.	Daniel	Babylon	Luke 3:1 + three-year ministry
Zechariah 9:9-17	480 B.C.	Zechariah	Jerusalem	Matthew 21:4,5; Mark 11:9,10; Luke 19:28-44; John 12:13-15
Zechariah 11:12,13	480 B.C.	Zechariah	Jerusalem	Matthew 26:14,15; 27:9
Zechariah 12:10	480 B.C.	Zechariah	Jerusalem	John 19:34-37

Prophecies of Jesus' Final Week

Many prophecies in the Bible link Jesus to the "ultimate Passover Lamb." There is incredible accuracy in the detail and precise timing of the prophecies of these events.

Prophecy or "Model"	Jewish Law	Fulfillment
• Passover Lamb (John 1:29,36)	• Lamb must be without blemish or defect (Exodus 12:3-5)	• Pilate (John 19:4) and Peter called Jesus "perfect" (1 Peter 1:18-21)
• "Anointed One"—"king"—will enter Jerusalem 483 years (69x7) after the decree to rebuild Jerusalem and the temple (Daniel 9:20-27). Adjusting for leap years and Jewish years, this equates to 173,880 days.[1,2,9,11,12]	• Lamb selected on tenth of Nisan **Selection of Passover Lamb**	• Triumphal entry: tenth of Nisan in the year of crucifixion[1,2] • The only time Jesus allowed Himself to be called "king"—fulfills Daniel's prophecy (Luke 19:38)
• Messiah will present Himself on a donkey (Zechariah 9:9-17)		• Rode a donkey into Jerusalem (Matthew 21:1-11; John 12:12-16)
• Melchizedek, king of Salem (Jerusalem), offers bread and wine to Abraham, who offers tithes to Melchizedek, honoring him (Genesis 14:18-20). • Joseph interprets dreams: baker (bread) had head severed (broken); cupbearer (wine) was redeemed (Genesis 40:1-19)	**Last Supper "Passover" of Jesus** • Unleavened bread (without sin) • Four symbolic cups of wine of Passover: 1. "Bring out" 2. "Delivering" 3. "Redemption" 4. "Take out"	• Jesus broke bread, describing it as His body "broken" for the world. Likewise after supper, referring to the third cup of wine (redemption cup), Jesus called it the cup of the new covenant in His blood—poured out for many. Final cup—for heaven (Matthew 26:26-29; Mark 14:22-25; Luke 22:19-21)

Prophecy or "Model"	Jewish Law	Fulfillment
• Silent when accused (Isaiah 53:7)	• Prisoner allowed to defend self—*required* to answer question of Messiahship	• Jesus said nothing except as required by law (Matthew 26:62-64).
• Obedient in time of humiliation (Isaiah 50)		• Obedient throughout trial
• Betrayed by friend (Psalm 41:9)	**Passover Lamb Killed** . . . . **Feast of Unleavened Bread Begins**	• Matthew 26:23; Mark 14:17; Luke 22:47
• 30 pieces of silver thrown on temple floor and given to a potter (Zechariah 11:12,13)		• Matthew 26:14,15; 27:9,10
• Crucified (Deuteronomy 21:23; Psalm 22:16)		• John 19:16-37; Matthew 27:51-66; Mark 15:33-37; Luke 23:45-49
• No bones broken (Psalm 22:17)	• No bones of lamb broken (Exodus 12:46, Numbers 9:12)	• John 19:32-36
• Pierced (Zechariah 12:10)	• Unleavened bread symbolizes "without sin"	• John 19:34,35
• Lots cast for clothing (Psalm 22:18)		• John 19:23,24; Matthew 27:35; Mark 15:24; Luke 23:34
• To die with wicked (Isaiah 53:9)		• Matthew 27:38; Mark 15:27; Luke 23:32
• Buried with rich (Isaiah 53:9)		• Matthew 27:57-60
• To be eternal, no decay of body—*resurrected* (Job 19:25; Psalm 16:10; 22)	**Feast of Firstfruits**	• "Easter" Sunday (John 20; Matthew 28; Mark 16; Luke 24)
	• Day after the Sabbath after Passover (Leviticus 23:11)	• Jesus—firstfruits (1 Corinthians 15:20)

Jesus' Own Prophecies

> The many prophecies of Jesus are
> extremely important because:
>
> 1. Perfect accuracy verifies His divinity (see pages 10–11),
> and
> 2. His prophecies provide important guidance (see page 44).

Prophecy from Jesus includes several prophecies immediately verified by people around Him (for example, Jesus told a centurion his servant would be healed—see Matthew 8:1-13). Other prophecies refer to judgment, to heaven, or to the end of the world. Jesus told His disciples that His precise prophecy of His death and resurrection was for reassurance that when the events happened they would know He was the Messiah (John 13:19), because the Jews realized that only God knows the future.

Prophecies of Jesus About His Own Death and Resurrection

- He would not again drink wine until He returns to establish a new kingdom (Matthew 26:27-29; Mark 14:23-25; Luke 22:17,18).

- One of His disciples would betray Him (Matthew 26:21; Mark 14:17-21; Luke 22:21,22).

- He did not come to abolish the Law, but to fulfill it prophetically (Matthew 5:17-20).

- His disciples would desert Him on the night of the Passover feast (Matthew 26:30,31; Mark 14:26,27).

- Peter would disown Him three times (Matthew 26:33,34; Mark 14:29,30; Luke 22:31-34).

- Prediction of His crucifixion (John 3:14-16).

- He would be "lifted up" (John 12:32-34).

- First prophecy of His death and resurrection (Matthew 16:21-28; Mark 8:31–9:1; Luke 9:21-27).

- Second prophecy of His death and resurrection (Matthew 20:17-19; Mark 10:32-34; Luke 18:31-34).

- Third prophecy of His death and resurrection (Matthew 26:2-5; Mark 14:1-9).

- Another prediction of the resurrection (John 2:13-22).

- More predictions about the resurrection (Matthew 26:32-34; Mark 14:28-31).

- Jesus' miraculous "sign" would be "like Jonah"— His resurrection after three days and nights (Matthew 12:39,40).

- If His body were destroyed, He would raise it in three days (John 2:19).

Prophecy Models of Jesus

As the previous pages indicate, prophecy can exist in the form of "types" or "models" of a particular person or event. History confirms Jesus' perfect fulfillment of the role of the Passover lamb in the strict observance of Jewish laws and customs. Other models ("types") of Jesus are found in the Bible as well.

Noah

Noah might be viewed as a "type" of Christ. "Righteous and blameless" (Genesis 6:9), he was assigned the task of "saving" a world filled with sin.

With eight people in the ark, Noah established a new beginning for mankind (even the number 8 itself is often used in the Bible to signify a "new beginning"). The Bible states that the ark came to rest on the mountains of Ararat on the *seventeenth day of the seventh month* (Genesis 8:4). In Noah's day, that was the month of Nisan. Later, God commanded Moses to establish Israel's "new beginning" by defining the month of Nisan as the *first month* (Exodus 12:1,2). The resurrection of Christ (also a "new beginning") occurred on the *seventeenth day of the month of Nisan*— the anniversary of the "new beginning" after the flood of Noah.[8]

Abraham and Isaac

The account of Abraham's near-sacrifice of Isaac is sometimes misunderstood. God clearly detests child sacrifice (Leviticus 18:21; 20:1-5). The event, however, provides a graphic prophecy of the later sacrifice of Jesus Christ.

The choice of words and details in the "sacrifice" of Isaac closely parallels the description of the sacrifice of Jesus some 2000 years later. It is a prophecy model.

The "Sacrifice" of Isaac
Compared to the Crucifixion of Christ

Birth was a miracle of God .... Genesis 21:1-8	Birth was a miracle of God .... Luke 1:31-35
Abraham (the father) provided .... Genesis 22:2	God (the Father) provided .... John 3:16
his one and only son, whom he loved, . Genesis 22:2	His one and only Son, whom He loved, ... John 3:16
as a sacrifice .... Genesis 22:2	as a sacrifice .... Matthew 3:17; Romans 3:25
Isaac carried the wood .... Genesis 22:6	Jesus carried the cross .... John 19:17
up a hill to the place of sacrifice .... Genesis 22:3,4	up a hill to the place of sacrifice .... John 19:18
Isaac (the son) was .... Genesis 22:2	Jesus (the Son) was .... John 3:16
"dead" for three days (in the mind of Abraham) .... Genesis 22:4; Hebrews 11:19	"dead" for three days .... Matthew 27:63,64
then was "resurrected" .... Genesis 22:13	then was resurrected .... Matthew 28; Mark 16; .... Luke 24; John 20
when a ram was substituted .... Genesis 22:13	as substitute for sin of the world .... Titus 2:14
Isaac "disappears" from Bible until united with bride .... Genesis 24	Jesus "disappears" from earth until united with bride (church) .... Revelation

The "Sacrifice" of Isaac and the Crucifixion of Jesus . . . Both on Golgotha?

Some biblical researchers have concluded that the site of the "sacrifice" of Isaac is exactly the same site where the crucifixion of Jesus took place 2000 years later.[8]

Proof: Prophecies About Christ Were Not Contrived

There is compelling evidence that the prophecies of Christ contained in the Old Testament could *not* have been contrived. In existence today are two sets of documents written hundreds of years before Christ.

The Dead Sea Scrolls

Hundreds of manuscripts, including all of the Old Testament books except Esther, were discovered in caves in the region of Qumran (near the Dead Sea) in 1947. Many of these works were written long before Christ, and some date as far back as 250 B.C.[10,13] Because the scrolls were hidden for centuries, they were left untouched and unaltered since they had been placed there in A.D. 70. All biblical prophecies of Christ are in the scrolls. Researchers have found almost no deviation in words or letters from the Hebrew versions of the Old Testament in use today. This provides us assurance that the documents were accurately duplicated over many centuries.

Jesus . . . the Messiah of Isaiah

When the Dead Sea scrolls were discovered in 1947, one particular scroll, the Book of Isaiah, was found in almost perfect condition in a clay container, though written long before Christ. The scroll can now be viewed in its entirety at the Shrine of the Book in Jerusalem. Isaiah provided more prophecies about the Messiah than anyone; they include the most detailed description of Jesus (Isaiah 53). It is so specific to Jesus of Nazareth that some Jewish sects have deleted it from Scripture. Yet the scroll in Jerusalem contains Isaiah 53 along with Isaiah's many other prophecies of Christ.

The Septuagint

In about 280 B.C., Jewish leaders decreed that seventy selected scholars would officially translate the Hebrew Scriptures into Greek (Greek was in common usage at the time). The *Septuagint* ("seventy") provides the best ancient scholarly translation from Hebrew to Greek of Holy Scriptures . . . completed at least 200 years before the time of Jesus. A few copies of this ancient document are still in existence,[7] providing more assurance that prophecies of Christ were complete and accurate before Jesus was born.

Were the Gospels Created to Match Prophecy?

A skeptic might ask, "Were the four Gospels written to match already-existing prophecy?"

Fact 1: The Gospel accounts were widely circulated in the lifetime of eyewitnesses. A lie would not stand this test.

Fact 2: Eleven of 12 apostles who *knew the truth* were executed (over a number of years) for their beliefs. Why would they die for a *known lie?*

Fact 3: Many other people died in support of the truth, some in the lifetime of eyewitnesses (seven million catacomb graves verify this). Why?

Fact 4: Paul, a prominent persecutor of Christians, gave up wealth and status, and later died to tell the story after seeing the risen Jesus. Why?

Prophecies of Israel and the Jews

There are many, many prophecies in the Bible concerning Israel and the Jewish people. Entire books have been written on selected prophecies. Here are some prophecy examples:

Covenants with Abraham

Name—Abraham's name would be great. Those blessing his descendents would be blessed, and those cursing them would be cursed (Genesis 12:2,3).

No name has become *great* in the same sense as that of the Jews. Though they were scattered from their homeland in A.D. 70 until the formation of Israel in 1948, the identity of the Jews has remained intact (that is, Jews live in many nations, yet are still known as Jews). Historically, *once separated from its homeland*, no other people has ever maintained its heritage and identity for more than about five generations.[7]

Slavery—Descendants of Abram (later named Abraham) would be strangers in a country not their own and would become enslaved for 400 years (Genesis 15:13-16). This occurred during the time from Joseph (circa 1880 B.C.) to Moses (circa 1450 B.C.).

Land—Abram was promised land reaching from the "river of Egypt" to the great river Euphrates—the land occupied by the Kenites, Kenizzites, Kadmonites, Hittites, Perizzites, Rephaites, Amorites, Canaanites, Girgashites, and Jebusites (Genesis 15:17-21). All these peoples were conquered by Israel, as indicated in the Old Testament books of history.

Conquering the Land

Several leaders of Israel received specific
prophecies of victories in the conquest of the land:

Moses
- Deliverance through the Red Sea (Exodus 14:13-21)... *Fulfilled:* Exodus 14:23-28
- Promise of defeat of Amalekites (Exodus 17:8-16) ..... *Fulfilled:* 1 Samuel 15:1-32;
  1 Chronicles 4:43

Joshua
- Promise of defeat of Jericho (Joshua 6:1-5) .... *Fulfilled:* Joshua 6:6-27
- Promise of defeat of Ai (Joshua 7:1–8:8) .... *Fulfilled:* Joshua 8:18-29
- Promise of defeat of northern kings (Joshua 11:1-6) .... *Fulfilled:* Joshua 11:7-15

Men of Judah
- Promise of defeat of Canaanites (Judges 1:1,2) .... *Fulfilled:* Judges 1:3-20

Deborah and Barak
- Promise of defeat of Sisera (Judges 4:1-11) .... *Fulfilled:* Judges 4:12-24

Gideon
- Promise of defeat of Midianites (Judges 6:11-24) .... *Fulfilled:* Judges 7

Saul
- Promise of defeat of Amalekites (1 Samuel 15:1-3) .... *Fulfilled:* 1 Samuel 15:4-9

David
- Promise of defeat of Philistines (1 Samuel 23:1-4) .... *Fulfilled:* 1 Samuel 23:5

Israel and the Jews
Prophecies of Exile

Exile to Babylon and Return[2]

Both Moses and Jeremiah prophesied about the Hebrew nation being exiled to Babylon (Jeremiah 25:9-11; Deuteronomy 28:49,50). Not only do their prophecies contain very detailed information, but they also set the stage for the introduction of "the Messiah."

Prophecy Elements . . .

1. A foreign nation, speaking a different language, would defeat the Hebrew nation (Deuteronomy 28:49).

2. They would destroy everything and not respect the elderly or pity the young (Deuteronomy 28:50,51).

3. They would lay siege to cities (Deuteronomy 28:52).

4. The Hebrews would resort to cannibalism (Deuteronomy 28:53).

5. Judah would be exiled to Babylon (Jeremiah 25:9-11).

6. After exile for *70 years* of "servitude," Babylon would be conquered and the Jews would return (Jeremiah 25:9-11).*

7. After *70 years* from the "desolation of Jerusalem" (Jeremiah 29:10-14), the final return from exile would be complete.*

*Note: Converting 360-day Jewish years to 365-day actual years yields exact fulfillment.

... And Their Fulfillment in History

722 B.C.—Assyria defeats the northern kingdom (Israel)

70 Yrs

606 B.C.—"Servitude of the nation"—Nebuchadnezzar, king of Babylon begins, the first siege of Jerusalem (Jeremiah 27:6-8; 29:10). Israel and King Jehoiakim of Judah are exiled along with key leaders, including Daniel (Daniel 1:1-4).

587 B.C.—"Desolations of Jerusalem"—the final siege of Jerusalem (see numbers 1,3,5 above). The barbarianism of the Babylonians is detailed in several places, including Lamentations (written in captivity): destruction (Lamentations 2:2-6—see number 2 above); siege (3:5—see number 3 above); the slaughter of young and old "without pity" (2:21—see number 2 above); cannibalism (2:20—see number 4 above).

537 B.C.—The Jews return at the decree of Cyrus 70 years after the first siege of Jerusalem (Ezra 1—see number 6 above).

70 Yrs

517 B.C.—The new temple is complete (see number 7 above).

The Second Exile Sets the Stage

The *second* exile, in A.D. 70, and the subsequent return of the Jews from all "directions" of the world were prophesied separately by Isaiah (Isaiah 11:11,12). Ezekiel also refers to this as a returning from all nations *(plural)*—(Ezekiel 37:21) and a unifying of Israel.

The establishment of the nation of Israel in 1948 and the return of Jerusalem to Jewish control in 1967 fulfill these prophecies. Like the first exile, the second exile set the stage for another coming of Christ. The timing of each was predicted using prophecies in Ezekiel and Leviticus.[8]

Prophecy Examples
People

Bible prophecies are of all types: information about *events* to occur, about *how* and *when* things will happen, and about specific *people*. Examples of prophecies include people such as:

Archaeology Confirms Cyrus's Decree

A stone cylinder was found that details many facts of Cyrus's reign, including the decree to rebuild Jerusalem and the temple.[10]

Cyrus (Isaiah 44:28)

Isaiah predicted 100 years in advance that both Jerusalem and the temple would be destroyed. At the time, Jerusalem was strong and the temple was a major landmark. He further predicted that a king named Cyrus would rebuild the temple—160 years before Cyrus was born.

Jesus—a Prophet "Like Moses"

The Hebrews were promised a great prophet "like Moses" (Deuteronomy 18:15,18). Jesus parallels Moses in many ways (Acts 3:20-23; Hebrews 3:2-6):

Moses	Jesus
• Baby hidden to escape Pharaoh's slaughter	• Baby hidden to escape Herod's slaughter
• Emerged from Egypt to redeem people	• Emerged from Egypt to redeem people
• 40 years' testing in desert	• 40 days' testing in desert
• Miracle worker	• Miracle worker
• Manna provided for food	• Bread provided for food
• Snake hung on pole to save lives	• Jesus hung on cross to save lives

Jerusalem and the temple were destroyed in 586 B.C. by King Nebuchadnezzar of Babylon. In 537 B.C., after Persia defeated Babylon, the Persian king, Cyrus, decreed that Jerusalem and the temple be rebuilt.

Jehoiachin—No Heir to the Throne?

Satan must have celebrated when Jeremiah prophesied that King Jehoiachin was cursed, and his *family line* would never again have the throne of Israel (Jeremiah 22:24-30). After all, he was in the *royal line of David*, the promised ancestor of the Messiah.

God solved this problem with the *virgin birth* of Jesus through Mary (also descended from David). The *legal line* came through Joseph, a direct descendent of Jehoiachin. So Joseph passed on the legal right of kingship to Jesus, despite not being His natural father.

Miscellaneous Prophecies about People

Joseph
- His brothers to bow down to him (Genesis 37:5-11) . . . *Fulfilled:* Genesis 42:6

Eli
- His sons Hophni and Phinehas to die on same day (1 Samuel 2:27-36) . . . *Fulfilled:* 1 Samuel 4:12-18

David
- Bathsheba's child to die (2 Samuel 12:14) . . . *Fulfilled:* 2 Samuel 12:19
- His wives violated by son, seen by nation (2 Samuel 12:11,12) . . . *Fulfilled:* 2 Samuel 16:22

Jezebel
- To be eaten by dogs (1 Kings 21:23) . . . *Fulfilled:* 2 Kings 9:30-37

Saul
- He and his two sons to die the next day (1 Samuel 28:16-19) . . . *Fulfilled:* 1 Samuel 31:6,8

Naaman
- To wash seven times in Jordan to be cured of leprosy (2 Kings 5:10) . . . *Fulfilled:* 2 Kings 5:14

Prophecy Examples
Places

Tyre[7] (Ezekiel 26:3-16)

In 586 B.C. (the eleventh year of the reign of Jehoiakim), the prophet Ezekiel was given a detailed prophecy regarding the powerful seaport of Tyre. At the time, Tyre was perhaps the greatest port in that part of the world. It could be equated to the New York or Hong Kong of today. The prophecy in Ezekiel outlines in detail several fates that awaited Tyre:

Archaeology Confirms Ezekiel

Stone tablets have been found with a nearly complete text of the book of Ezekiel dating from 600–500 B.C. (the time of Ezekiel). This verifies the existence of the prophecy long before its fulfillment.

1. Nebuchadnezzar would destroy the city on the mainland.

2. More than one nation would come against it.

3. The city would be flattened like the top of a bare rock.

4. The area would become a site for spreading nets.

5. Stones and timbers would be thrown into the water.

6. The city would not be rebuilt.

7. Nearby rulers would give up their thrones.

Fulfillment in History—In 586 B.C. Nebuchadnezzar destroyed the city on the mainland, forcing people to the island portion of the city (see number 1 above). In 332 B.C. Alexander the Great began a siege of the island city. In order to reach it, he scraped the stones and timbers from the mainland city into the water to form a great causeway (see numbers 2,3,5 above). Due to the successful siege, many neighboring rulers surrendered to Alexander without a fight (see number 7 above). Today the ancient mainland portion of Tyre remains a flat rock where local fishermen dry nets (see numbers 4,6 above).

Edom and Petra[7]

Once a key trade route and a city
stronghold, it would be:

- Unpopulated (Isaiah 34:13; Jeremiah 49:18) . . . *Fulfilled:* now barren, unpopulated

- Conquered by heathen (Ezekiel 25:4) . . . *Fulfilled:* in the sixth century B.C. by Assyrians

- Conquered by Israel (Ezekiel 25:14) . . . *Fulfilled:* conquered by Hyrcanus, Simon of Gerasa

- Desolate to Teman (Ezekiel 25:13) . . . *Fulfilled:* Teman (on border) is the only populated city

- Inhabited by animals (Isaiah 34:10,11; Ezekiel 35:7) . . . *Fulfilled:* now home of lions, leopards

- Void of trade (Isaiah 34:10; Jeremiah 49:17) . . . *Fulfilled:* now no people, no trade

Samaria[7]

- To fall violently (Hosea 13:16) . . . *Fulfilled*: Fell 331 B.C. to Alexander the Great, 107 B.C. to Hyrcanus

- To become a planting place (Micah 1:6) . . . *Fulfilled*: great city converted to gardens

- Ruins, stones thrown in valley (Micah 1:6) . . . *Fulfilled*: foundations discovered—building ruins had been thrown into valley

Gaza[7]

- To become "bald" (Jeremiah 47:5) . . . *Fulfilled*: Old city site now completely covered with sand (Note: The new city of Gaza is in a completely different location.)

Prophecy Examples
Events

Prophecy of events was highly significant because it confirmed which people were prophets of God (for example, Joseph's prediction of plenty/famine—Genesis 41:1-32; Daniel's prophecy to Nebuchadnezzar—Daniel 4:1-37). The accuracy of the Bible provides us with the same assurance that it is from God.

The Jews Return to Israel
(Genesis 13:14,15; Isaiah 11:11,12; Ezekiel 37:21)

The dramatic return of the Jews to Israel on May 14, 1948, is powerful evidence of the prophetic accuracy of the Bible. No skeptic can deny:

- The prophetic claims that the Jews would be returned to the land (Israel)
- The unlikelihood that Jewish identity would survive for centuries (see page 34)
- The incredible odds against the modern world allowing the return of the Jews
- The fact that Israel now exists, in spite of all odds

Isaiah emphasizes this return to the land by prophesying it as a *second* return from *all corners of the earth* (Isaiah 11:11,12).

Desecration of the Temple by Antiochus Epiphanes
(Daniel 8:9-14)

In about 535 B.C., Daniel recorded prophecies of a coming ruler who would:

- Overthrow Israel (Daniel 8:10)
- Establish himself as ruler and "God" (Daniel 8:10,11)
- Take away daily sacrifices (Daniel 8:11)
- Desecrate the temple (Daniel 8:11)

Reconsecration of the temple was to occur:

- 2300 "evenings and mornings" afterward (Daniel 8:13,14)

This prophecy marks a milestone in Jewish history. Antiochus Epiphanes overthrew the priest in 171 B.C. and established himself as ruler and self-proclaimed "god." He then prohibited sacrifices in the temple, persecuted the Jews, and desecrated the sanctuary with the sacrifice of a pig on the altar (an event abhorred by the Jews), which sparked the Maccabean revolt. Reconsecration of the temple took place on December 25, 164 B.C.—commemorated today by the Jewish holiday of Hanukkah. And it occurred 2300 days after the beginning of the desecration, which started with the overthrow of the high priest.

Importance of "Contemporary Prophecy"

Skeptics may claim that prophecies of events that occurred during a prophet's lifetime may have been invented after the fact. This presumes that holy Scripture (the written record) was not truly regarded as "holy." History refutes such a claim.

Contemporary prophecy provided witnesses of those prophesied events assurance that prophets had divine inspiration. Future prophecy of these prophets could then be viewed as reliable. Examples of contemporary prophecy include:

Prophecy	*Fulfillment*
• Seven years plenty, seven years famine (Genesis 41:1-32)	Genesis 41:45-57
• Josiah to be born, to sacrifice pagan priests (1 Kings 13:1-3)	2 Kings 23:15-17
• Drought to plague Israel (1 Kings 17:1)	1 Kings 18:36-45
• Rain to come at Elijah's request (1 Kings 18:41)	1 Kings 18:45
• Treasure carried to Babylon (Jeremiah 20:5)	2 Chronicles 36:18

Common Questions

What Is the Most Important Prophecy?

The Bible doesn't rank prophecies by degree of importance. For any certain individual, however, prophecies affecting eternal life might be regarded as the most important. Considering the Bible's prophetic perfection—and considering Jesus' prophetic perfection—it would be foolish to ignore prophecies about eternity made by either.

Key prophecies that greatly affect every man, woman, and child:

1. Heaven is real, wonderful, and eternal (Matthew 13:44,45).

2. Hell is real, horrible, and eternal (Matthew 10:28; 18:8,9; Mark 9:43; Luke 16:23-31).

3. Every person will exist in heaven or hell eternally (Matthew 25:31-46).

4. Everyone who follows Jesus will go to heaven (John 3:16).

Do Other Holy Books Contain Accurate Prophecy Like the Bible?

No other holy book has the prophetic accuracy of the Bible. Most holy books, including those of the major world religions, are noticeably void of prophecy. Since prophecy is a standard by which to "test everything" (see pages 10–11), one would expect works *not* from God to avoid prophecy (or to contain errors).

A few holy books of some religions contain limited attempts at prophecy, with results that fall far short of God's perfect standard. A few examples include:

The Book of Mormon, Pearl of Great Price, Doctrines and Covenants—

- *False prophecy:* Jesus to be born in Jerusalem (Alma 7:10), which is defined to be a distinctly separate city (1 Nephi 1:4). History and the Bible confirm Bethlehem as Jesus' birthplace.[4]

- *False prophecy:* "After the Jews believe Jesus is the Messiah, they will return to the land of Israel" (2 Nephi 10:7). In 1948 the Jews returned to Israel, still rejecting Jesus.[6]

- Information claimed to be historical within the *Book of Mormon* has not been confirmed as true. The Smithsonian Institution flatly rejected the book as historical.[4]

- *The Book of Abraham*, supposedly translated by Joseph Smith, was proven fraudulent.[6]

- A temple was to be built at a consecrated location in Jackson County, Missouri ("Zion"), "within a generation" of 1832 (Doctrines and Covenants, 84:5,31; September 1832). The city (Zion) was "never to be moved" out of that place (97:19, August 1833, and 101:17-21; December 1833). Over 150 years have passed (several generations) and no temple is there.[6]

Watchtower (Studies in Scripture)[5]—

- (2:101)—1914 to be the year of the "battle of the great day of God Almighty" (Revelation 16:14).

- (1914 edition)—"End of the world" date changed to 1915.

- (7:62)—Date changed to 1918.

- (7:542)—Date changed to 1920.

- (Miscellaneous other publications)—Date of the end of the world was repeatedly changed to 1925, 1942, 1975, 1980. . . .

Is Jeane Dixon a Prophet?[7]

Famous for the prediction that John F. Kennedy would be elected and die in office (*Parade*, 1950), Jeane Dixon would hardly qualify as a biblical prophet.

First, the odds of this prediction were not amazing . . . one chance in five.

Second, many of her prophecies were wrong:

- World War III did not happen in 1954.

- Jackie Kennedy married Aristotle Onassis the day after Dixon predicted she would never remarry.

- The Vietnam Conflict did not end in 1966, but rather in 1975.

What Does Prophecy Say About the End of the World?

About one third of biblical prophecies deal with the end of the world. The most important point is the outcome: God's victory over evil (Revelation 20:7-10).

Does Prophecy Reveal Life After Death?

The 100 percent accuracy of historical prophecy provides assurance that prophecy about life after death is also true. Jesus prophesied that those who follow Him will have eternal life with God. Those who don't, won't (Mathew 27:51-53; John 3:16; 5:18-24; 14:6-9; Acts 4:12; Colossians 1:15-23; Hebrews 10:26-31).

How Can We Ensure the Right Relationship to Go to Heaven?

When Jesus said not all who use His name will enter heaven (Matthew 7:21–23), He was referring to people who think using Christ's name along with rituals and rules is the key to heaven. A *relationship* with God is *not* based on rituals and rules. It's based on grace and forgiveness, and the right kind of relationship with Him.

How to Have a Personal Relationship with God

1. **B**elieve that God exists and that He came to earth in the human form of Jesus Christ (John 3:16; Romans 10:9).

2. **A**ccept God's free forgiveness of sins through the death and resurrection of Jesus Christ (Ephesians 2:8-10; 1:7,8).

3. **S**witch to God's plan for your life (1 Peter 1:21-23; Ephesians 2:1-5).

4. **E**xpress desire for Christ to be director of your life (Matthew 7:21-27; 1 John 4:15).

Prayer for Eternal Life with God

"Dear God, I believe You sent Your Son, Jesus, to die for my sins so I can be forgiven. I'm sorry for my sins, and I want to live the rest of my life the way You want me to. Please put Your Spirit in my life to direct me. Amen."

Then What?

People who have sincerely taken the above steps automatically become members of God's family of believers. A new world of freedom and strength is available through prayer and obedience to God's will. New believers can build their relationship with God through the following steps:

- Find a Bible-based church that you like, and attend it regularly.

- Try to set aside some time each day to pray and read the Bible.

- Locate other Christians to spend time with on a regular basis.

God's Promises to Believers

For Today

But seek first his kingdom and his righteousness, and all these things [things to satisfy all your needs] will be given to you as well.
—Matthew 6:33

For Eternity

Whoever believes in the Son has eternal life, but whoever rejects the Son will not see life, for God's wrath remains on him.
—John 3:36

Once we develop an eternal perspective, even the greatest problems on earth fade in significance.

Notes

1. Anderson, Sir Robert. *The Coming Prince*. Grand Rapids, MI: Kregel Publications, 1984.

2. Eastman, M.D., Mark and Missler, Chuck. *The Creator Beyond Time and Space*. Costa Mesa, CA: The Word for Today, 1996.

3. *Encyclopedia Britannica*. Chicago, IL: 1993.

4. Martin, Walter. *Kingdom of the Cults*. Minneapolis, MN: Bethany House Publishers, 1996.

5. McDowell, Josh and Stewart, Don. *The Deceivers*. San Bernardino, CA: Here's Life Publishers, Inc., 1992.

6. McDowell, Josh and Stewart, Don. *Handbook of Today's Religions*. Nashville, TN: Thomas Nelson, Inc., 1983.

7. McDowell, Josh and Wilson, Bill. *A Ready Defense*. San Bernardino, CA: Here's Life Publishers, Inc., 1990.

8. Missler, Chuck. *Footprints of the Messiah*, audiotape. Coeur d'Alene, ID: Koinonia House Inc., 1995.

9. Missler, Chuck. *The Magog Invasion*. Palos Verdes, CA: Western Front Publishing, 1995.

10. Muncaster, Ralph O. *The Bible—General Analysis—Investigation of the Evidence*. Mission Viejo, CA: Strong Basis to Believe, 1996.

11. Phillips, John. *Exploring the World of the Jew*. Neptune, NJ: Loizeaux Brothers, 1993.

12. Rosen, Moishe. *Y'shua*. Chicago, IL: Moody Bible Institute, 1982.

13. Shanks, Hershel, ed. *Understanding the Dead Sea Scrolls*. New York: Vintage Books, 1993.

14. Walvoord, John F. *The Prophecy Knowledge Handbook*. Wheaton, IL: Victor Books, 1990.

Bibliography

Archer, Gleason L. *Encyclopedia of Bible Difficulties*. Grand Rapids, MI: Zondervan, 1982.

Life Application Bible. Wheaton, IL: Tyndale House Publishers, and Grand Rapids, MI: Zondervan Publishing House, 1991.

McDowell, Josh. *Evidence That Demands a Verdict*. Nashville, TN: Thomas Nelson, Inc., 1979.

McDowell, Josh and Wilson, Bill. *He Walked Among Us*. Nashville, TN: Thomas Nelson, Inc., 1993.

Missler, Chuck. *Feasts of Israel,* audiotape. Coeur d'Alene, ID: Koinonia House Inc., 1995.

Missler, Chuck. *Walk Through the Bible,* audiotape. Coeur d'Alene, ID: Koinonia House Inc., 1995.

Muncaster, Ralph O. *Jesus—Investigation of the Evidence*. Mission Viejo, CA: Strong Basis to Believe, 1996.

Shepherd, Coulson. *Jewish Holy Days*. Neptune, NJ: Loizeaux Brothers, 1961.

Strauss, Lehman. *God's Prophetic Calendar*. Neptune, NJ: Loizeaux Brothers, 1987.

Smith, F. LaGard. *The Daily Bible in Chronological Order*. Eugene, OR: Harvest House, 1984.

Youngblood, Ronald F. *New Illustrated Bible Dictionary*. Nashville, TN: Nelson, 1995.